T0365353

My
D.r.e.a.m. Journal
- For Student Leaders

30-Day Authentic Journaling

Clarity. Purpose. Direction

Coach Lara

Print information available on the last page.

Rev. date: 05/30/2018

To order additional copies of this book, contact:
Xlibris
0800-056-3182
www.xlibrispublishing.co.uk
Orders@ Xlibrispublishing.co.uk

PRESENTED TO

BY

OCCASION

CONTENTS

INTRODUCTION VII
a. *How I Started My Own Dream Journal.* VII
b. *Why Do I Need A Dream Journal?* XII
c. *What Is Authentic Journaling?* XV
d. *How To Begin* XVII

PART 1

10 DAYS OF WISDOM
(Practicing Listening) 1

PART 2

10 DAYS OF RESTRAINT
(Practicing Self-Control) 14

PART 3

10 DAYS OF BECOMING
(Seeing Results) 28

CONCLUSION 43

NOTES 44

To my children: Francine, Franklyn and Richard,

for allowing me be the best mum I could be.

With all my love!

To **The Servant Leaders** - *my past and current students and mentees,*

thank you for letting me learn with and through you.

INTRODUCTION

How I Started My Own Dream Journal

You're probably wondering:

"Why do I need a Dream Journal" or, *"What is Authentic Journaling, anyway?* I have answered these two questions and more in subsequent pages. But first, let me tell you how I started with **My *Own* Dream Journal**.

Authentic Journaling for me began in 2000, after the birth of my last child. Months before then, I dreamt and *saw* that I was going to have a baby boy. I also *received* the names to call him in that dream. It was almost as if the personality and purpose of this child was being revealed to me before he came. Different from how it happened with my two other children, whom I grew to know and love, I felt like I knew this child already! As a young woman, I would absent-mindedly scribble my thoughts and dreams in my diaries; but by this time, I needed more space for the volume of inspiration that was coming to me - every day. So I bought my first notebook or journal a few days before my son was born and my first entry, on September 1 2000, would be his names, as I *received* them.

From this time on, journaling my dreams became somewhat of a *ritual*. The images became sharper and the voice clearer. I found it exhilarating to wake up in the early hours of the morning and hear a Voice speak into my heart, almost like a whisper, about the day that hasn't yet begun; or about my life and the lives of people and things I cared about. Convinced that this was beyond my own finite mind; and that I was actually *receiving* valuable and very important information from a *Source Higher* than me, I wanted more – everyday! I had always *seen* images in my head, even as a child, but this was different; this was a much *Higher Intelligence* than was known to or possible for me. It was so much more wisdom than I could attain on my own. Sometimes, the messages would come as warnings, other times as ideas and solutions, and some other time, as faces or names of people to speak to, or be wary of. There was no hiding from this *Source* – He was always there, every single morning when I woke up. I just had to do two things – *wait and listen!*

Now after nearly 18 years, I am totally "addicted" to Authentic Journaling! And this is a *good addiction*, because armed with fore-knowledge, I am never out of ideas and rarely confused about what I want. I have clarity about my life's purpose and where I am headed. Why? Because all has been or is being given to me! I love the fact that I can live my life more accurately and on purpose. I especially love the sense of assuredness, the stability and harmony that Authentic Journaling brings to my soul. I want you to experience the same stability and harmony in your soul. I want you to have the assurance which produces *a confidence that knows that ALL WILL BE WELL!* So, I am sharing with you here, FOUR HABITS which I developed to help me stay focused and consistent with my practice of Authentic Journaling. I hope they help you too and open up *your untapped world* as they did mine.

My First Dream Journal

Some of my other old Journals

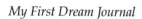

My Authentic Journaling Habits

Habit 1 - Rise Up Early!

To succeed in any area of life, you would need to develop healthy habits that support your behaviour in that area. Rising early was probably the most difficult adjustments I had to make because I loved my sleep, whether as a teenager or as a full grown adult. But "Early" is where the secret hides! There is something empowering about rising early and *dominating* your day before everybody else starts. "Early" for me meant before anyone else around me woke up. It meant, before I picked up my phone to check for text messages; before I got on social media, or called anyone. "Early" was and still is between 4 and 5.00am. For you, it may be 6.00am, but whatever time you choose, it must be before you get into the busyness of the day; before you expose your mind to all that is going on around you; before social media, radio or television. The essence of Authentic Journaling is to focus your mind on something purposeful, first thing in the morning, before your mind gets dragged into the confusion of the day.

This was not an easy discipline for me and it won't be for you either, but the gains far outweigh the sacrifice. Some say, "Early" is when God speaks. I say, *God speaks all the time*, but "**Early**" is when we are most likely to hear accurately. Perhaps He also honors the element of sacrifice that comes with rising early to seek wisdom and direction, when most people are still sleeping.

Habit 2 - Tarry to Think!

My *Tarry-to-Think* time usually takes between 10-15 minutes. Once I become fully awake, I get up and pour myself a glass of warm lemon-infused water to cleanse my system and recline on my favorite couch. I gather my thoughts and try to recall what I might have seen or heard in my sleep. Then I ask what they mean and what I'm supposed to do with them. Lastly, I try to *capture* in **My Dream Journal** what becomes clear or the responses I'm getting to my questions. Often, the thoughts and ideas that come to me during this time are helpful in planning my day, but sometimes they have come to prepare me for the days and months ahead.

Habit 3 - Read and Write!

I see my Bible as a book of answers not as a religious book. Every day, I take 30-45 minutes, sometimes one hour after my *Tarry-to-Think* time, to dig into it for knowledge and Wisdom. This is the kind of wisdom not taught in any school, but *breathed* into the recipient from the *Higher Source*. As I study, I write down thoughts, questions or quotes as they come to me. Then I mutter or say out loud the verse or words from the Bible that strike me as I read. I would repeat these 2-3 times to let them sink into my soul and then write them down. Usually while this is going on or soon after, thoughts will begin to come into my mind about varied things and I would write them down as they come, or sketch them out if they were images.

I refrain from telling you whether or not to study the Bible or how to do it. This is a decision you must arrive at yourself because you see the gains of doing so. But I will tell you this: every time I have sought answers or ideas on what to do, I have found them through this practice. They may or may not come from the Bible verses I'm reading, but they always come during or after my *Read-Write* practice. So you can be rest assured that this is one sure way of finding answers – answers you will not get anywhere else! As you begin to *receive* directly from *the Source*, the Bible becomes your point of reference. It will either corroborate or refute what you're *hearing* and *seeing*. If it doesn't confirm your thoughts or images, then you do not want to act on them.

Habit 4 - Go Back to Move Forward!

My 4th habit or practice is to *Go Back* in order *to Move Forward!* From time to time, I would pick up my old journals in search of answers I may already possess. If I feel stuck or something happens that feels like a *déjà vu*, I *Go Back* to see if I might have seen it coming; and more often than not, I would have! I also go back to evaluate myself and to appreciate God for being my *Internal GPS*. I check to see how many of the thoughts and ideas I have utilized and how many I have left un-actioned. I tick those things that I *saw* coming and actually happened, and I cancel those that might have been the figment of my imagination. Lastly, I *Bring Forward* the things yet to be done and set a plan to achieve them. *Going Back to Move Forward* helps me move forward with precision, because I now have the benefit of foresight or fore-knowledge. On the whole, I am amazed and humbled by the amount of *treasure* poured into me through this simple but deliberate act of spending time in meditation, every day. By now I'm sure you know that the idea for what you hold in your hand *(MDJ)* came through this practice. Now, imagine what *treasure* is waiting to come out of you!

So far, I have kept nearly 40 journals and these are the habits and practices that have helped me to stay focused and consistent. **Trust**, **Focus** and **Consistency** are the three most important attributes you will need to make this work for you: Trust in the truth that God loves you and has the Blueprint for your life[1]. Many people are confused and unhappy today because they have not discovered the Blueprint. Every builder needs a Blueprint to build a house; you need a Blueprint to build your life! Once you have established **Trust**, you now need to **Focus** on YOU. Focus on building your life – one block at a time! Push out all distractions and focus on finding your *Reason For Being*. You do this by **Consistently** practicing the disciplines recommended here, to help bring the results you need. Everyone can do a good act once in a while; but only very few people stay true to doing the good that they know. Few people succeed in life because they are the few that stay true - the few that stay CONSISTENT! Be one of them!

By all means, develop whatever habits and practices you prefer, but feel free to adopt my own FOUR and stay true to whatever you decide. If you seek wisdom and want clarity and direction for your life; if you desire to live your life's purpose, this is a good place to start. *MDJ* will take you on a journey to Self-Discovery! God wants more than anything else, to lead and guide you. He wants to show you His plan for your life and give you the best ideas for success. But you must be willing to develop the disciplines necessary for you to get what you want. You must be ready to trust Him, because one day He might tell you to go left when it *makes sense* to go right.

Now, let me warn you that, things may not happen immediately. You may not hear or see anything for the first day or even week. But if you persist and stick to your daily routines and habits, it will surely happen. I have a hard time listening to someone I do not have a relationship with – even when they speak at the top of their voice. I have to make an effort to pay close attention to hear them. However, if I care about someone, I could merely look into their eyes and *hear* even the words they're not speaking. Why? Because I care…I know them…I love them!

This is how it is *listening* for that **Voice Within** you. Though God is speaking, and constantly too, many do not hear, because they haven't taken the time to develop a relationship with Him. They are not tuned into Him to learn how He speaks, what He says, what He likes or dislikes. No one wants to be *"besties"* with someone they didn't know or agree with[2]. To become close friends with someone, you would first make an effort to understand their ways, and then love and respect them for who they are. It works the same way with God. You first want to "court" His friendship, get to know Him and make Him your confidant. Then, you will begin to see things from His perspective and trust that He wants the best for you. **My Dream Journal** will help you do this. As you journal in it every day, you will start to develop a close relationship with your Creator, and He will in turn begin to guide and direct you[3]. You will know His heart concerning you and the plan He has for you. You will become more confident in who you are and what you can achieve. So that, even when it seems like you cannot hear Him, you will have a *knowing* so strong in your heart and *know* just what to do.

Now, if you're ready for this special journey and will work diligently through **My Dream Journal (MDJ)** for the next 30 days, say this short prayer before continuing:

Dear God,

I want to know You. I want to have a close relationship with You. I surrender my heart to you and ask You to fill it with Your knowledge and Your wisdom. Be my Friend and Confidant. I know You think the best of me and I trust You to guide and direct me, every day of my life. Lead me and teach me how to lead others, just like you. Make my life extra-ordinary.

Thank You, in Jesus name. Amen!

(Signature & Date)

*"The wise counsel God gives when I'm awake
is confirmed by my sleeping heart.
Day and night I'll stick with God;
I've got a good thing going and I'm not letting go"*[4]
~ King David

Why Do I Need A Dream Journal?

Sometimes during my youth events, some brilliant young people would walk up to me and ask that I mentor them to become Public Speakers. They want to speak and be heard and I love that! But I also wonder whether *"Speaking"* is the real dream of these young people, or whether it is someone else's dream they admire and want for themselves. I ask if they want to become Public Speakers because "speaking" appears glamorous, or if indeed they have an authentic message to speak about. I want to tell them to be patient; to listen *first* to the *Voice of Direction* within them and to take some time to figure out what their own unique message is. The first step to succeeding as a leader is **Self-Discovery.** No leader is truly able to show another the way until she has first travelled that way herself!

Another question I get asked frequently, by my young and not so young friends is: ***"How Can I Hear God?"*** Perhaps this is the utmost question I seek to answer with **My Dream Journal**.

I speak to my audiences about my "gift" of perception or *"spiritual insight"*. While I realize this is a special gift which comes *almost* naturally to me and to several other people, I also know that there is a *skill element* to every "gift". The skills and disciplines we develop around our "gifts" are what make them seem effortless and easy. These skills can be developed or cultivated, to one degree or another, by adopting the right disciplines, even where there is no apparent "gift". As a young girl I could *see* or *sense* things and would sometimes "predict" them before they happened. However, the visions quite often left me in fear or confusion because I had no understanding of what to do with them or where they came from. I also lacked the maturity and character required to operate in this kind of "gift", at that time.

When I started raising my children, I realized that they also were quite perceptive. They blurted out ideas or solutions to issues we were dealing with as a family, and many times, without realizing what they had said. My experience has been the same with other young people I have worked with over the years. Some as little as 6 years old, would time and again, say the wisest and most peculiar things; almost as if they embodied *Someone* else. It was obvious that these words and ideas did not originate from them. Their words were *inspired* - by a *Higher Source...a Higher Intelligence.*

With these experiences, I came to two conclusions:

a. *That, God speaks to everyone, but not everyone hears Him;*

b. *That, young people (children & youths), have an uncanny ability to hear and receive from God more accurately than adults.*

As I reached these conclusions, I also imagined…...

How different the world would be if thousands, maybe millions of young leaders – Student Leaders - all over the world, could tap into this Ultimate Source of Knowledge and Wisdom. What would happen if the next generation of leaders were directly inspired and led <u>by God</u> as they lead others? What would happen if each of these young leaders had a Blueprint for their lives; and if they pursued and lived that Blueprint without deviating? How different would the world be?

You have to forgive me, but I am an *Incurable Dreamer*! Many good things have happened to and for me after I dreamt or envisioned them. I hope you will join me by becoming another *Incurable Dreamer* that this world needs. The world seeks answers! So let's give it more dreamers - dreamers like Dr Martin Luther King, who will through their dreams, visions and imaginations, provide the answers – answers that will *make the impossible, possible*!

It may be different in your part of the world, but in my culture in Nigeria, young people are usually on the receiving end of communication – they are told what to do, when to do it and how to do it: what university attend, what course of study to choose and sometimes, who to or who not to marry. They are told *what to think* but not taught HOW TO THINK! Even though a lot of this is gradually changing, more still needs to change. I believe parents all over the world should give more autonomy to their teenagers and young adults and empower them to make their own decisions, because this is where ingenuity and creativity comes from. However, as a parent myself, I share the concerns of many parents who have a hard time letting go; who fear that their young ones might make wrong choices and throw their lives away. That is every parent's worst nightmare!

This is why I am writing to you as a Young Leader. If you want more autonomy, then you have to buckle up! More autonomy or more freedom comes with more responsibilities and the willingness to develop the right disciplines that will help you THINK right and ACT sensibly. Experience has shown me that young people albeit inexperienced and largely irrational, are inherently wise when **led or guided** to think for themselves and seek answers from within them. My job with *MDJ,* is to help you arrive at the place I call *"Responsible Autonomy"*.

When you learn *the Art of Thinking*, you **become** empowered to make your own decisions and are ready to be responsible for your choices. You learn to depend on the Ultimate Source of Guidance and Direction. You become confident to discuss your *options* with your parents or teachers rather than wait for them to tell you what to do. You take the reins of your life and you begin to lead it. I want to equip you as a young leader, to THINK for yourself; to pull out the answers God has put inside of you; to hear the *Voice of Direction* clearly and learn how to heed it. I want help open up your spirit to receive God as your Guide[5]; so you can lead your life successfully and help others do the same. To achieve these, I am providing you with the following **3 Tools** in *MDJ*:

1. *A **Way** to initiate deep THINKING – which will provoke your dreams, visions and imaginations;*

2. *The **Space** that allows your individuality and uniqueness to come out as you receive from your Creator, who visits you daily and as an <u>individual</u>; and*

3. *A **System** to record and retrieve these inspirations or messages for immediate or future use.*

The world needs *a new generation of leaders;* leaders who will be true to themselves and lead from the heart. I believe that generation is yours! The goal of *MDJ* is to help you become that great leader that the world seeks. For that to happen, you must *first* lead yourself. You will only succeed at leading others when you have succeeded at leading yourself. YOU my friend, are your most difficult follower!

> *"Hear this, young men and women everywhere.....*
> *you are needed now more than ever before.*
> *Take up the mantle of change....for this is your time!!"*
> *~ Sir Winston Churchill.*

Winston Churchill made this call to the youths of his generation. But it is ripe and relevant even today. So I say to you dear Student Leader, **this is your time!** Let the change that this world needs begin with and in you. Start leading your life so you can begin to lead your generation!

"To Thine Ownself Be True"
~ William Shakespeare.

What Is Authentic Journaling?

Authentic Journaling is how we talk *(or in this case, write)* to ourselves when no one is watching. You've probably said to someone before: ***"C'mon Get Real!"?*** Well, **Authentic Journaling** is how YOU *Get Real* - with yourself! It is when you take off the *"mask"* and let your guard down; when you allow that weak or *unsightly* part of you show.

I see many young people today love to express themselves freely. They love to talk freely to people, and allow people to talk freely to them, or *at them*. However, it seems they seldom speak or listen to *themselves*. Better still, they very rarely allow themselves to hear *"the Gentle Whisper"*; the *"Still Small Voice"*[6] from within them. While they do not seem to have any problem listening to every voice around, they hardly listen to their own voices! It would appear that many are lost in the struggle to become who someone else wants them to be. In a desperate bid to *be like, sound like* or *look like* someone else, they lose sight of who they were created to be!

Living real and authentically in this fast-paced world is becoming somewhat *'endangered'*! The "populism phenomenon" is costing many youths their true identities. Very few are keen on discovering who they really are. Many seem satisfied acting like *everyone else*. But *"everyone else"* is *No One….No Identity….No Uniqueness….No DNA* – and that's pretty boring! There is however a lot of interests these days in becoming celebrities! And I see nothing wrong with that in itself, but at what cost? To what end? Who or What do you allow to shape the trajectory of your life? Who influences your decisions? TV personalities? Actors? Musicians? Politicians? Is your happiness tied to the many *'Likes'* you get or DON'T get on social media? Who or What is your greatest influence?

I doubt that anyone would knowingly tailor their lives after the similitude of these "celebrities" if they were *consciously* aware that many of them hardly represent the best models of character. Yet, if all I see as a young person are these "celebrities" as we all do on TV, movies and the social media; then that's the highest standard that I'm likely to believe possible; after all as they say: *"monkey see monkey do"*!

This is the era where it seems unwholesome behaviors attract the most attention and are too quickly glamorized. Role modelling has become less about character and virtue and more about popularity and who can make the loudest noise! Sadly, too many young people are unwittingly adopting these as enviable and even *acceptable standards of behaviour.* This unfortunate trend makes me very unhappy and keeps me up at night.

I'm not sure which is worse for me: the level of moral decadence in our societies, or the lack of sensitivity towards it by many.

Just because something is "popular" or "acceptable" to a lot of people should not make it right or acceptable to you![7]

My dream is to see more young people like you, all over the world give keen attention, deep and careful thought to **Who** they truly are, **Who** they want to become and **What** it is they were put on this planet to achieve. This is where True Success comes from. The truth my friend is, you can only be the *counterfeit* of someone else! But I would rather you took some time every day with yourself and with your Creator, to discover your ***True and Authentic Self*** and the reason for which He put you here. Then you will receive the strength to proudly ***give that REAL YOU as a gift to the world!***

So now, don't settle for less than YOU! Don't stoop to the level of someone else's opinion of you or accept their standard of success as yours. Your Creator invested so much in making you an **Original**. Don't short circuit the greatness He embedded in THIS ORIGINAL - by pursuing the flawed image of a Counterfeit. A Tailor needs a pattern to make a dress, a Designer creates something new; something that has never existed, from the *inspiration* he receives. Start receiving the *inspiration* you need to create *Your Own Pattern!* Be Your Own Life's Designer! Let **My Dream Journal** provide you with the inspiration and space you need to ***Design Your Best and Most Authentic Life***!

Remember, THERE IS NO ONE ELSE LIKE **YOU**! And it's that unique **YOU** that I'm cheering on!

Coach Lara

"Ideas are like slippery fish.
If you don't spear them with a pencil they get away"
~ Earl Nightingale.

How To Begin

MDJ offers you a 3 Step process of 10 Days each, to train your spirit or your sub-conscious how to *receive* the highest knowledge and wisdom possible. Each day starts with a unique quote taken from the Book of Proverbs to jolt you to think. The Book of Proverbs consists of basic common sense sayings, idioms and instructions, which if applied consistently, are capable of making *anyone* wise and successful in whatever they do. By starting your day - *everyday* – ruminating over these quotes, you are preparing your *thinking mind* – your subconscious mind, to *receive* the inspiration that is getting ready to come to you. I suggest that you follow my example and start your day early, perhaps half an hour to one hour earlier than usual. Be ready to devote the first 15-20 minutes of each morning and the last 15-20 minutes of each night, to doing this. After *thinking* over the day's **Quote**, you are then presented with 5 **"Dream Questions"**. Try not to spend more than 2-3 minutes on each question or a total of 20 minutes at a time (morning and evening). Start and end your day *authentically* journaling in **MDJ**, by allowing yourself complete freedom of expression. Write down exactly how you're feeling and what is topmost on your mind. Starting each morning with a *Capture* of your thoughts and ending the day with a *Review* of your actions will help you keep track of what is happening in and through you.

The daily **Quotes** help to awaken your subconscious mind, while the 5 **Dream Questions** will give your conscious mind power to *receive* and translate what is coming from your subconscious, where truth and authenticity reside. Your conscious is fed or influenced by your sub-conscious. This process is called **Spiritual Thinking** - where you engage your subconscious with the *Mind of God*[8]; so that your subconscious receives information that is true, authentic and relevant to your wellbeing and the purpose for which He created you. The process does not need to be an intense or a laborious one. It should not take too much time either. You would not have to work it or force yourself to think or make it happen. You only need to practice *listening* and *waiting,* after meditating on the daily quotes and attempting the 5 **Dream Questions.** You are not **the Source**; you are simply the *Receptacle* or the *Container* through which *the Source* pours His wisdom. You are lending or releasing yourself to be used to bring to Earth the thoughts of Heaven. The thoughts, ideas or solutions do not come from you; they come to and *through* you. So be patient and position yourself to receive!

The daily discipline of journaling helps you to develop the patience you need to connect your mind to the *Higher Intelligence* – the *Spiritual Intelligence* of God. Meditating on each day's quote and answering the questions that follow, make it easier to tune your mind to **"Receptive Mode"**. To meditate, start by reading the daily quotes quietly, then aloud, muttering the words to yourself slowly 2-3 times, to allow your subconscious to receive and record them. The questions have been designed to penetrate your conscious mind and pull answers or ideas from your sub-conscious. So it may take a little while for the answers to come to you. And if answers are not forthcoming for one question, move to the next. You may find yourself quietly reflecting on your most prominent thought during the course of the day, until the answer or idea drops. Allow that to happen naturally without trying to force an answer. The answer will come to you when you least expect it! The more you practice this process, the keener your listening and receptive abilities will become.

As you become diligent with the *Practices of Listening and Restraint,* what will start to come to you will be beyond you; beyond all you could possibly think or imagine[9]. Remember, you do NOT have the answer and you're NOT **the SOURCE**; you **RECEIVE** the answer and you're the **RECEPTACLE**! Sometimes instead of words, you may receive images, or an *apparition* of something or someone, so that the image is not clear, but you know you saw something. And if you are someone who prefers to represent what you're *hearing* and *seeing* with images, this would be the time to turn to the **Sketch Pages** provided at the end of each stage of the Journal. Make sure to draw or sketch what you're *seeing* as soon as possible. If you do not, like Earl Nightingale said, it may fade out of your memory and become difficult to retrieve once the day's activities begin.

The purpose of *MDJ* is to equip and empower you to receive spiritual insights and guidance for your life's journey. The Journey of Life is a long and arduous one and you will need all the help you can get! We all do. You will never be 100% clear about all that will come to you, but you will have enough assurance and peace to keep moving forward, confidently. Trust your instincts and keep moving forward; your path becomes clearer as you go! If you would do this diligently, I guarantee that you will be more certain about your life and what lies ahead of you than most people your age. You will be guided into all that you need to do, and will receive strength to live that extra-ordinary life already *prepared for you.*[10]

When He, the Spirit of truth comes, He will guide you into all the truth….
He will tell you what is yet to come.[11]

Part 1

----

10 DAYS OF WISDOM
(Practicing Listening)

The Value of Wisdom is to Help You Succeed[12]

$\mathcal{P}$*racticing Listening* will help you to embrace humility. It will prepare your mind to **learn** new things; to **unlearn** the habits and attitudes that are not helping you; and to **relearn** things you thought you knew. Humility is when you recognize and accept that you do not have all the answers; that things are not always as they seem. It is that attribute that enables you to depend on another *(in this case, God)*; for help and guidance. Listening changes your posture from *giving* your opinion to *receiving* someone else's opinion. Here, it enables you to see life from God's perspective. When you *practice listening* to God, you will be operating at a much higher level of awareness; a much higher level of consciousness.

Wisdom is your ability to choose and apply the knowledge you have, <u>correctly</u>. Many people are knowledgeable but very few are wise. *Knowledge is not enough!* Knowledge only becomes power when it is applied correctly and takes you further in life. If the knowledge you have causes you to regress, then it has not translated into wisdom.

My hope as you begin your *Practice of Listening* is that the power that wisdom supplies will be delivered to you; to move your life further and to bring you success. Now go ahead and get Wisdom; it's the most important thing!

Day 1
Listen, I Have Important Things To Tell You[13]

Your Dream Questions:

1.   What's on Your Mind Today?

_____

_____

_____

2.   What Do You See? *(See Sketch Page for more space)*

_____

_____

3.   What Do You Hear?

_____

_____

_____

4.   What Could You Do To Make This Day A Great Day?

_____

_____

_____

5.   What Do You Need Help With?

_____

_____

_____

Day 2
I'll Share My Heart With You And Make You Wise[14]

Your Dream Questions:

1. **What's on Your Mind Today?**

_____

_____

_____

2. **What Do You See?** *(See Sketch Page for more space)*

_____

_____

3. **What Do You Hear?**

_____

_____

_____

4. **What Could You Do To Make This Day A Great Day?**

_____

_____

_____

5. **What Do You Need Help With?**

_____

_____

_____

Day 3

Listen to Me, For All Who Follow My Ways Are Joyful[15]

Your Dream Questions:

1.   *What's on Your Mind Today?*

_____

_____

_____

2.   *What Do You See?* *(See Sketch Page for more space)*

_____

_____

3.   *What Do You Hear?*

_____

_____

_____

4.   *What Could You Do To Make This Day A Great Day?*

_____

_____

_____

5.   *What Do You Need Help With?*

_____

_____

_____

Day 4

All Who Listen To Me Will Live In Peace, Untroubled By Fear[16]

Your Dream Questions:

1.   ***What's on Your Mind Today?***

_____

_____

_____

2.   ***What Do You See?*** *(See Sketch Page for more space)*

_____

_____

3.   ***What Do You Hear?***

_____

_____

_____

4.   ***What Could You Do To Make This Day A Great Day?***

_____

_____

_____

5.   ***What Do You Need Help With?***

_____

_____

_____

Date: ---/---/-----

Day 5
The Wise Listens And Becomes Even Wiser[17]

Your Dream Questions:

1.   *What's on Your Mind Today?*

_____

_____

_____

2.   *What Do You See?* *(See Sketch Page for more space)*

_____

_____

3.   *What Do You Hear?*

_____

_____

_____

4.   *What Could You Do To Make This Day A Great Day?*

_____

_____

_____

5.   *What Do You Need Help With?*

_____

_____

_____

Your Dream Questions:

1.   *What's on Your Mind Today?*

_____

_____

_____

2.   *What Do You See?* *(See Sketch Page for more space)*

_____

_____

3.   *What Do You Hear?*

_____

_____

_____

4.   *What Could You Do To Make This Day A Great Day?*

_____

_____

_____

5.   *What Do You Need Help With?*

_____

_____

_____

Day 7

I Will Teach You Wisdom's Ways And Lead You In Straight Paths.[19]

Your Dream Questions:

1.   *What's on Your Mind Today?*

_____

_____

_____

2.   *What Do You See?* *(See Sketch Page for more space)*

_____

_____

3.   *What Do You Hear?*

_____

_____

_____

4.   *What Could You Do To Make This Day A Great Day?*

_____

_____

_____

5.   *What Do You Need Help With?*

_____

_____

_____

Day 8
When You Walk, You Will Not Be Held Back.[20]

Your Dream Questions:

1.   What's on Your Mind Today?

_____

_____

_____

2.   What Do You See? *(See Sketch Page for more space)*

_____

_____

3.   What Do You Hear?

_____

_____

_____

4.   What Could You Do To Make This Day A Great Day?

_____

_____

_____

5.   What Do You Need Help With?

_____

_____

_____

Your Dream Questions:

1.   *What's on Your Mind Today?*

_____

_____

_____

2.   *What Do You See?* *(See Sketch Page for more space)*

_____

_____

3.   *What Do You Hear?*

_____

_____

_____

4.   *What Could You Do To Make This Day A Great Day?*

_____

_____

_____

5.   *What Do You Need Help With?*

_____

_____

_____

Day 10
Wise Choices Will Watch Over You.[22]

Your Dream Questions:

1. **What's on Your Mind Today?**

_____

_____

_____

2. **What Do You See?** *(See Sketch Page for more space)*

_____

_____

3. **What Do You Hear?**

_____

_____

_____

4. **What Could You Do To Make This Day A Great Day?**

_____

_____

_____

5. **What Do You Need Help With?**

_____

_____

_____

Part 2

----

10 DAYS OF RESTRAINT
(Practicing Self-Control)

I said to myself: "I will watch what I do and not sin in what I say.
I will hold my tongue." -King David[23]

*R*estraint is that attribute that keeps you in check; it is what saves you from yourself. When applied as Self-control, it demonstrates your conquest over *Self*! This is where you learn to weigh your actions before you take them; or where you *think* before you think. **Practicing Restraint h**elps you decide before you have to. As you journal along for the next 10 days, you will discover that the most difficult person you will ever lead is YOURSELF! You will start to learn how to pause to think; when to stop, or when to simply say "NO"! This is where you begin to really lead *yourself*!

Self-Control is your ability pull or stop yourself from doing things you feel like doing, but recognize that they may have grave consequences for you or those you care about. You choose to do this by pulling the brakes on yourself; not needing anyone looking over your shoulders, telling you what to do. This is where you prepare to take charge of your life! The next 10 days will help you think over things you probably never gave serious thoughts to before. This is how you beat peer-pressure and stand on your convictions. You think and you decide who you want to be, so no one needs to tell you who you should be. This *Practice* will help you become confident and comfortable in your own skin. Instead of allowing yourself to be influenced negatively, you become the Positive Influence on others! You *make your own mind up* and give no one the power to make it up for you.

Practicing Restraint can be difficult at first, but it gets easier as it becomes your choice – your convictions. It is better to deny yourself now than to live a life of regret, as you come face to face with the consequences of your wrong choices.[24] This section will help you develop the strength of character that enables you to apply necessary caution to your irrational thoughts and feelings. I know restraining oneself is counter-intuitive to how most young people think; it was to me too. And that is exactly what this Journal is set out to help you with – NOT think like every other young person out there, but to think at a much higher level; to allow yourself to be distinguished; and set apart for greater things.

Desiring "freedom" or wanting to do as you please is a natural reaction to the growth you are experiencing. It is every young person's way of seeking autonomy because you want to take charge of your life, and that's a good thing. We were all created to want that! The problem is if you're not prepared and equipped for that "independence" that you crave, your wrong choices in the time of immaturity could lead you into undesirable paths that may keep you stuck for years to come. So while it is a good thing to be "independent" and be "free" to do as you please, it is also worthwhile to seek guidance and adopt *self-leadership*.[25]

The price for *Independence* is <u>Responsibility</u>. You can't be independent and be irresponsible at the same time. Independence will expose you to judgement and the consequences of your actions. *Practicing Restraint* helps to minimize your exposure.

My hope is that as you meditate and journal through this section, you will learn to how to master your emotions rather than be a slave to them; that you will receive the strength to do what is right rather than what is popular. The *listening* skills you have developed in **Part 1** will be put to test here, but every time you pass each test thrown at you, know that you are being transformed into the REAL YOU that God intended when He created you.[26]

- -

"You're the master of your fate, the captain of your ship."
– William E. Henley

To Learn, You Must Love Discipline; It Is Stupid To Hate Correction.[27]

Your Dream Questions:

1.   *What's on Your Mind Today?*

_____

_____

_____

2.   *What Do You See?* *(See Sketch Page for more space)*

_____

_____

3.   *What Do You Hear?*

_____

_____

_____

4.   *What Could You Do To Make This Day A Great Day?*

_____

_____

_____

5.   *What Do You Need Help With?*

_____

_____

_____

Your Dream Questions:

1. **What's on Your Mind Today?**

_____

_____

_____

2. **What Do You See?** *(See Sketch Page for more space)*

_____

_____

3. **What Do You Hear?**

_____

_____

_____

4. **What Could You Do To Make This Day A Great Day?**

_____

_____

_____

5. **What Do You Need Help With?**

_____

_____

_____

Day 3
The Prudent Carefully Consider Their Steps.[29]

Your Dream Questions:

1.   *What's on Your Mind Today?*

_____

_____

_____

2.   *What Do You See?* (See Sketch Page for more space)

_____

_____

3.   *What Do You Hear?*

_____

_____

_____

4.   *What Could You Do To Make This Day A Great Day?*

_____

_____

_____

5.   *What Do You Need Help With?*

_____

_____

_____

Day 4

Sensible People Control Their Temper.[30]

Your Dream Questions:

1. **What's on Your Mind Today?**

_____

_____

_____

2. **What Do You See?** *(See Sketch Page for more space)*

_____

_____

3. **What Do You Hear?**

_____

_____

_____

4. **What Could You Do To Make This Day A Great Day?**

_____

_____

_____

5. **What Do You Need Help With?**

_____

_____

_____

Date: ---/---/-----

Your Dream Questions:

1.   *What's on Your Mind Today?*

_____

_____

_____

2.   *What Do You See?* *(See Sketch Page for more space)*

_____

_____

3.   *What Do You Hear?*

_____

_____

_____

4.   *What Could You Do To Make This Day A Great Day?*

_____

_____

_____

5.   *What Do You Need Help With?*

_____

_____

_____

Day 6

Spouting Off Before Listening… is Shameful And Foolish.[32]

Your Dream Questions:

1.   What's on Your Mind Today?

_____

_____

_____

2.   What Do You See? *(See Sketch Page for more space)*

_____

_____

3.   What Do You Hear?

_____

_____

_____

4.   What Could You Do To Make This Day A Great Day?

_____

_____

_____

5.   What Do You Need Help With?

_____

_____

_____

Day 7
A Wise Person Stays Calm Even When Insulted.[33]

Your Dream Questions:

1.   What's on Your Mind Today?

_____

_____

_____

2.   What Do You See? *(See Sketch Page for more space)*

_____

_____

3.   What Do You Hear?

_____

_____

_____

4.   What Could You Do To Make This Day A Great Day?

_____

_____

_____

5.   What Do You Need Help With?

_____

_____

_____

Your Dream Questions:

1. ***What's on Your Mind Today?***

_____

_____

_____

2. ***What Do You See?*** *(See Sketch Page for more space)*

_____

_____

3. ***What Do You Hear?***

_____

_____

_____

4. ***What Could You Do To Make This Day A Great Day?***

_____

_____

_____

5. ***What Do You Need Help With?***

_____

_____

_____

Date: ---/---/-----

Day 9
It's Better To Have Self-Control Than To Conquer A City.[35]

Your Dream Questions:

1.   *What's on Your Mind Today?*

_____

_____

_____

2.   *What Do You See?* *(See Sketch Page for more space)*

_____

_____

3.   *What Do You Hear?*

_____

_____

_____

4.   *What Could You Do To Make This Day A Great Day?*

_____

_____

_____

5.   *What Do You Need Help With?*

_____

_____

_____

Day 10

If You Fail Under Pressure, Your Strength Is Too Small.[36]

Your Dream Questions:

1. ***What's on Your Mind Today?***

_____

_____

_____

2. ***What Do You See?*** *(See Sketch Page for more space)*

_____

_____

3. ***What Do You Hear?***

_____

_____

_____

4. ***What Could You Do To Make This Day A Great Day?***

_____

_____

_____

5. ***What Do You Need Help With?***

_____

_____

_____

Date: ---/---/-----

Part 3

----

10 DAYS OF BECOMING
(*Seeing Results*)

Come, Follow Me,
And I Will Show You How to Fish For People![37]

This is where a lot of action is required from you. Your informed decisions will be backed by calculated steps. The personal change you have worked for, for the last 20 days will now begin to show. You are listening and learning; you're gaining wisdom and being inspired to pursue greatness. There is no true success without sacrifice, so hopefully, you are also *denying* yourself of pleasures you would ordinarily not think twice about. You're *practicing* silence when all you feel like doing is shouting! You're learning how to take control of who you are and determine who you want to be.

Now, get ready to emerge into a BRAND NEW YOU! You will **BECOME** someone different from whom many around you knew….*someone different from whom you knew!* You are now on the driver's seat of your life and allowing yourself to have a firm say in who you become. This is when you will start to align your actions with God's idea of who you truly are. Only He has the Blueprint for your life; and I'm sure He has begun to show you that Blueprint. He will also empower you to put the pieces together, like a puzzle – one piece at a time. You will have more clarity about who you truly are and what your mission on earth is. No one has the right to put the pieces of your life together for you; they don't have the Blueprint, **you do!** Even God will not put the pieces together for you, but He will strengthen and guide you to do it yourself. You must now make up your mind to do *what you need to do to become who you want to become.*

"Following" implies that you recognize and accept that you need help; that you can't do it alone. Asking for help does not mean you have failed; it means you are not alone; **and you are not!** So, keep following the lead of the *Teacher Within* you; ask for help every day and take every step He guides you into. As you take action every day towards your daily goals, your growth will become evident to all, and like a Butterfly you will start to *metamorphose*. You will transform from *Egg to Caterpillar,* to *Pupa* and then to a strong beautiful *Butterfly!* The change you are experiencing will also impact those around you. But remember, **Growth is Continuous**. So don't be in a hurry; allow your growth to happen daily and continuously. It will be a systematic process – a process that never ends; a process that is certain to take you from one level to another.[38]

Date: ---/---/-----

Your Dream Questions:

1. **What's on Your Mind Today?**

_____

_____

_____

2. **What Do You See?** *(See Sketch Page for more space)*

_____

_____

3. **What Do You Hear?**

_____

_____

_____

4. **What Could You Do To Make This Day A Great Day?**

_____

_____

_____

5. **What Do You Need Help With?**

_____

_____

Date: ---/---/-----

Walk With The Wise And You'll Become Wise.[40]

Your Dream Questions:

1.   *What's on Your Mind Today?*

_____

_____

_____

2.   *What Do You See?* *(See Sketch Page for more space)*

_____

_____

3.   *What Do You Hear?*

_____

_____

_____

4.   *What Could You Do To Make This Day A Great Day?*

_____

_____

_____

5.   *What Do You Need Help With?*

_____

_____

_____

Day 3

Guard Your Heart Above All Else;
It Determines The Course Of Your Life.[41]

Your Dream Questions:

1.   *What's on Your Mind Today?*

_____

_____

_____

2.   *What Do You See?* *(See Sketch Page for more space)*

_____

_____

3.   *What Do You Hear?*

_____

_____

_____

4.   *What Could You Do To Make This Day A Great Day?*

_____

_____

_____

5.   *What Do You Need Help With?*

_____

_____

Your Dream Questions:

1.   ***What's on Your Mind Today?***

_____

_____

_____

2.   ***What Do You See?*** *(See Sketch Page for more space)*

_____

_____

3.   ***What Do You Hear?***

_____

_____

_____

4.   ***What Could You Do To Make This Day A Great Day?***

_____

_____

_____

5.   ***What Do You Need Help With?***

_____

_____

_____

Your Dream Questions:

1. ***What's on Your Mind Today?***

_____

_____

_____

2. ***What Do You See?*** *(See Sketch Page for more space)*

_____

_____

3. ***What Do You Hear?***

_____

_____

_____

4. ***What Could You Do To Make This Day A Great Day?***

_____

_____

_____

5. ***What Do You Need Help With?***

_____

_____

_____

Your Dream Questions:

1. ***What's on Your Mind Today?***

_____

_____

_____

2. ***What Do You See?*** *(See Sketch Page for more space)*

_____

_____

3. ***What Do You Hear?***

_____

_____

_____

4. ***What Could You Do To Make This Day A Great Day?***

_____

_____

_____

5. ***What Do You Need Help With?***

_____

_____

_____

Day 7
Put GOD In Charge Of Your Work,
Then What You've Planned Will Take Place.[45]

Your Dream Questions:

1.   *What's on Your Mind Today?*

_____

_____

_____

2.   *What Do You See?* *(See Sketch Page for more space)*

_____

_____

3.   *What Do You Hear?*

_____

_____

_____

4.   *What Could You Do To Make This Day A Great Day?*

_____

_____

_____

5.   *What Do You Need Help With?*

_____

_____

Your Dream Questions:

1.   *What's on Your Mind Today?*

_____

_____

_____

2.   *What Do You See?* *(See Sketch Page for more space)*

_____

_____

3.   *What Do You Hear?*

_____

_____

_____

4.   *What Could You Do To Make This Day A Great Day?*

_____

_____

_____

5.   *What Do You Need Help With?*

_____

_____

Day 9
Choose A Good Reputation...Being Held
In High Esteem Is Better Than Silver or Gold.[47]

Your Dream Questions:

1.   *What's on Your Mind Today?*

_____

_____

_____

2.   *What Do You See?* (See Sketch Page for more space)

_____

_____

3.   *What Do You Hear?*

_____

_____

_____

4.   *What Could You Do To Make This Day A Great Day?*

_____

_____

_____

5.   *What Do You Need Help With?*

_____

_____

Day 10

Speak Up For Those Who Cannot Speak For Themselves.[48]

Your Dream Questions:

1.   What's on Your Mind Today?

_____

_____

_____

2.   What Do You See? *(See Sketch Page for more space)*

_____

_____

3.   What Do You Hear?

_____

_____

_____

4.   What Could You Do To Make This Day A Great Day?

_____

_____

_____

5.   What Do You Need Help With?

_____

_____

_____

I Believe in You!

Hopefully by now, you have discovered how to use your intuition and judgement. You're probably better able to make decisions based on your convictions rather than on your feelings. Emotions can be powerful, but they are also fickle and you can't always rely on them. You can however rely on and base your actions on the truths that you know. And when you do, your emotions will fall in line. You will always receive strength to rise above your feelings, but whether you ask for and receive that strength is entirely up to you. **Dream Question** No. 5 is what reminds you to ask for help, every day. We all need help, so ask – DAILY and God will point you to whom He has chosen to bring it to you. No matter what you're going through, you're never alone, unless you choose to be. Help is always at hand: you just need to ask!

Now, don't limit yourself to just the initial 30-Days of *MDJ*. Keep going over your thoughts and adding new insights daily as they come, or get a second copy of *MDJ* until you are satisfied with your progress. From now on, the *Plumbline* of your judgement and decisions will be guided by a stronger sense of *right and wrong*. Your decisions concerning your present and future actions will now be made from a place of careful thought and planning, rather than on your whims. The journey will by no means be easy and you will need to make some tough choices There will be grey areas; so when you're not sure what to do, do the best that you know and trust God to make everything right, for your good.[49] **You are NEVER alone!**[50]

I know you can do this! Coming along this far tells me you are serious about your life; that you want more out of this life! I believe in you and I'm confident that you will do all you can to bring out the *treasures within you*. You're the Leader this world is waiting for; so go and change your world!

I am eager to learn of your transformation and would love to hear from you.
Email me and tell me how **My Dream Journal** is working for you.
Best wishes my Friend!

Coach Lara

Websites: www.mydreamjournal.com/laraejizu.com
Email: coachlara@laraejizu.com

Notes

1. *See Jeremiah 29:11, Psalm 139:17 NLT*

2. *See Amos 3:3 NLT*

3. *See Proverbs 3:6; Isaiah 30:21 NLT*

4. *Psalm 16:7 (MSG Bible)*

5. *See Psalm 32:8 NLT*

6. *See 1Kings 19:11-13*

7. *See Romans 12:2 NLT*

8. *See 1Corinthians 2:16 NLT*

9. *See Ephesians 3:20 NLT*

10. *See Jeremiah 1:5; Jeremiah 29:11 NLT*

11. *John 16:13 NLT*

12. *Ecclesiastes 10:10 NLT*

13. *Proverbs 8:6 NLT*

14. *Proverbs 1:23 NLT*

15. *Proverbs 8:32 NLT*

16. *Proverbs 1:33 NLT*

17. *Proverbs 1:5 NLT*

18. *Proverbs 18:15 NLT*

19. *Proverbs 4:11 NLT*

20. *Proverbs 4:12 NLT*

21. *Proverbs 2:16 NLT*

22. *Proverbs 2:11 NLT*

23. *Proverbs 39:1 NLT*

24. *See Proverbs 5:12-14*

25. *See Proverbs 11:14 NLT*

26. *See Jeremiah 1:5 NLT*

27. *Proverbs 12:1 NLT*

28. *Proverbs 29:15 NLT*

29. *Proverbs 14:15 NLT*

30. *Proverbs 19:11 NLT*

31. *Proverbs 13:16 NLT*

32. *Proverbs 18:13 NLT*

33. *Proverbs 12:16 NLT*

34. *Proverbs 17:27 NLT*

35. *Proverbs 16:32 NLT*

36. *Proverbs 24:10 NLT*

37. *Matthew 4:19 NLT*

38. *See 2Corintians 3:18 NLT*

39. *Proverbs 15:33 (MSG Bible)*

40. *Proverbs 13:20 NLT*

41. *Proverbs 4:23 NLT*

42. *Proverbs 6:3 NLT*

43. *Proverbs 4:25 NLT*

44. *Proverbs 16:1 NLT*

45. *Proverbs 16:3 (MSG Bible)*

46. *Proverbs 6:6 (MSG Bible)*

47. *Proverbs 22:1 NLT*

48. *Proverbs 31:8 NLT*

49. *See Romans 8:28 NLT*

50. *See John 14:18 NLT*

Printed in the United States
By Bookmasters